BEFORE THE GRAVE

Selected Poems

D.S. POORMAN

EDITED BY KENT FIELDING

Radial Books

Also by D.S. Poorman
Macky Dunn's Got Nothing to Lose
Once Removed
Somewhere There's a Place
The Largest Poetry Book in the World

Copyright © 2021 by D.S. Poorman
All rights reserved.

The poems in this book though they may reference historical events, real locations, and/or real people, are fictitious.

No part of this publication may be reproduced, distributed or transmitted in any form or by any means, without prior written permission of the publisher.

Kent Fielding would like to specifically thank Laura Loran for reading and rereading drafts of this manuscript and giving suggested revisions. He would also like to thank Ryan Masters for his feedback and suggestions on various poems in this book. And thanks to Tricia Yost for her attention to detail and help to make this book happen.

Cover Design by Jen Walters Petry, 2020. jenwaltersstudio.com

Published by Radial Books
radialbooks.org
Beyond the Grave / D.S. Poorman, edited by Kent Fielding, 1st ed.

ISBN: 978-0-9984146-7-6

I have ever since seemed to myself broken off from mankind: a kind of solitary wanderer in the wild of life, without any direction, or fixed point of view; a gloomy gazer on a world to which I have little relation.

SAMUEL JOHNSON

CONTENTS

PERSONAL 1
    Personal 3
    At Night, The City Is Absent 4
    Lost In White 6
    Running 8
    A Foreign Hand 12
    An Old Cave 14
    Night Passing 17
    Curator 19
    Mascaron 20
    Childlike 21
    Unexpected 22
    Kent, ... 23

THE WEIGHT OF BROKEN GLASS 25
    Sunday Morning 27
    The Fire Below 29
    Continental Sonnet 30
    Another 31
    The Lover 32
    Aphonia 33
    An Account Of My Birth 34

KICKBALLS AND OVERGROWN LAWNS 37
    Winter 39
    Violence 40
    Kickballs And Overgrown Lawns 41
    Something That Happened Before I Thought Of You 42
    Sober 43

Everywhere, Something 44
Black Harvest 45
On Value 46
I've Become The River 47

THE DANCE OF THE BLACK WASPS 49
Too Late, The Windy Evening Has Come 51
Evolution 52
Radio Tower 53
The Run Of The Squirrel 55
Table Prayer 56
Cicada 57
Autumnal 58
Ohio River 59
The Night Rain 60
Prayer 61
Toad As Orphan 62
Dragons 63
The Singing Of The Wasps 65
Avalanche 66
Kind Eulogy 67
Like Trees Like Water 68
Red 69
Midnight Prayer 70
The Dance Of The Black Wasps 71

NO BOTTOM 73
The State Fair 75
On The Radio After The Storm 79
The McAlpine Locks 80
No Bottom 82

DISTORTED HISTORY 85
The Day I Stopped Writing 87
Undermining 89
The Meaning Of Work 92
A Song For Marcia On Mother's Day 97
The Poor Addition 98
Give My Love To Father 103
Distorted History 105

FLAME 107
Echo 109
After The Hospital 110
An Immense Waiting 111
Sheer White 114
Skeleton 115
Slowly 116
Veins 117
Veins II 118
Veins III 119
Flame 120
Before The Grave, ... 122
Epilogue 124

AFTERWORD by Kent Fielding 125
ABOUT THE AUTHOR 139

PERSONAL

PERSONAL

I am perpetually caught off guard
by mean people and the beauty of simple clouds
floating through the melting orange of sunset.
Took a one-way ticket to sexuality, when
three-foot-four, seventy-two pounds,
just turned eleven-years-old,
and suffered bedroom abuse from a neighbor.
Slept with anyone I could charm from their clothes
until, thirty-four, when I suddenly
realized what had happened, and
the vast ocean of the human heart
opened before me like the clapped shut wings
of a hidden butterfly stirred awake by a gentler breeze.
In possession of many truths like tiny colorful paintings
dotting the vast plane of a high white wall,
but consider patience the premier virtue
in pursuit of the sweet comfort of happiness.
Can meet for coffee, devoid of pretensions,
will not try to impress, great understander of pain,
talkative, a little bit goofy, movie lover, laughing.

AT NIGHT, THE CITY IS ABSENT

I am always amazed when the sun comes up
in yawning orange and fire yellow,
and I, a small animal, am there to see it.
I am stunned as if by a needle from a gun,
and for a brief moment believe,
am horrified to believe, that I came first.
A moment ago, I was in darkness,
belonging to other things: to peace
of a million lightless lights and settled dust.
A quiet bed stuffed with miles of wet earth.
The rain that beat a thousand beats a second
upon the leaking roof and absence of birds.
The only proof that anything at all moves
in the ponderous solitude before the sun,
before it rises, is a dog's imagination,
and a hill obscured by faulty eyes that drops
away like an ocean on the horizon,
and the sound of trees bearing with the wind.
Myself, I do not exist in the night.
Am part of it instead. Enlivened by it.
Know it, touch it, feel it, want it,
and am amazed when it goes away.
When the sun comes up and reveals to me,
my naked body, my hard penis in my hand,
the cat I saved, the room I built, the rocks I moved
with my broken back, my words carved in tree trunks,
opened up like flowers by the burning sun.
Its power to erase all that I have imagined,
and replace it with this world before me,
in torment and selfish anger, this world
of yours called daytime, the waking hours
when truth is made apparent by reality.

I am always amazed when the sun comes up,
and I am there to see it, as if I came first,
and made the city happen far, far away.

LOST IN WHITE

They said if you were lost
among the bunged blanket of the fall hills,
out among the sumac spreads,
and tangled in the gooseberry,
that you should stay in one place
and wait for their net of gauze
to come and hide you from the dark.

They said conventional wisdom
was the more you wandered to find yourself,
the more you would go away,
and my little legs tried to believe them,
but beneath my feet was the home
I would build away at Retreat
among the Pennyroyal trails, the ranger's signs.

They said you should lay in the mother's milk
and waft your arms like a silly duck.
You could scream from that spot,
because the hills were friendly,
and they would take your pleas
of belonging, hold them in their veins
feed them to the great inner-working.

As if the soles of our feet
hidden in the gray and orange Saucony
were little ports plugging us
into the motherboard of our ship,
this consciousness welling up like
camp fire hazy in a waking vision.
They said if you were lost in white,

the safest thing was to stop,
call out your name. That in time
it would come to you, the safety
of numbers and the wall of understanding.
And if I would have listened to them,
heard they had been there before,
forever I could have stood

among that halcyon of my shared bedroom
in that rough complex,
those meals my mother squeezed from
her busy checkbook,
that father, I would try to open
like a trick safe that has no combination,
as I called my own name over and over.

They said if they weren't around
and nothing seemed familiar
you should freeze
as soon as you came to this realization.
I tried to believe them.
But I had no patience for being found.
The hidden path crunching under foot.

RUNNING

I found my best friend
running cross country in high-school,

taking the hills together
after class beyond the tennis courts,

and the diamonds scattered
like softballs during batting practice,

along the verdant run of urban park,
and the rut of the fescue to dirt,

the souls in tandem
beating a frame along the trails.

We'd tail each other,
mists of sweat beneath the blazing,

around the sharp turns.
We'd dig our cleats into the gruff

of fern and wire fence,
spaghetti dinners the night before

each race, every Saturday,
after the long run of the week.

There was no end to
the romance of the pack.

The common charge
toward the common goal.

Sometimes as I broke from them
along the rumble strips of root,

wearing out my shoes
in a fierce desire to win,

I'd open up my stride,
my step as long as dreams,

or as complete as the nighttime sky,
the sober stars, the burned-out mass,

the hurling giants of my childhood.
My brother and I

placed a blanket for our backs
along the driveway tar

to watch a meteor storm
for the first time in our lives.

I looked up, innocent, asked my father
if Dan and I would be able

to hear them as they fell
in darkness ripped by light.

He told me those flames
were hundreds of miles up,

and if I were to hear one
then I should run like hell

from the cages of steel,
the empty bottles,

the brown puddles,
run like hell, child,

the advice of this man
with no friends.

So, there I was
in my high school years

galloping like a Thoroughbred
around Seneca Park

with the light of Heaven
chasing me without a sound,

the breathing of the herd
at my shoulder,

my friend like a second skin
to hold me in this world,

of Tulips purple with bruise
the yellow lily of drunk livers,

the black ants of lungs,
the knotted laces swinging,

as I kicked and pushed forward,
full of the hunt,

for a place to draw a slow breath,
to forget the call of others,

a place to write it out
that I have been running

that wide dip and loop
beyond the expressway,

passed the bridal path
and the 15th Hole at Seneca,

for half my life now,
and the great light flew overhead

long ago, its mad noise really, a whisper
I missed, a glow I've come to chase.

A FOREIGN HAND

There is no object in my house
more valuable than the space
upon which it sits.
There are three tons of rock beneath
the once plowed dirt
upon which my basement rests.
There is a footer of concrete
and a slab floor cracked along
a line where the earth shifted.
There is a bed beneath my pillows,
a stand to hold my old TV,
and a shelf beneath the books I read in 1993.
I've washed the dirty dishes and
put them out to dry by the sunlight
through the window beneath the sky.
There is a voice beneath my throat
choked with tears and black as dye,
and children above the street playing with dirt bikes.
I hear them yell and shout, calling names
their mothers should not hear,
and beneath every man is a boy.
Mine is speaking to me, whispering a painful song
into the conch of my ears.
And, I think there must be an ocean
beneath every desire to die,
a black crescent moon beneath the fighter's eye.
Mine, they have swollen shut,
and last night I could not see
that there are people in the soil and soil in the tree.
There is a past, a foreign hand
once upon my child's thigh,
and an old man's cock standing high.

But there is no object in my house
more valuable than the space
upon which it sits.
And any man is a wasted boy
who moves forward
meaning only to forget.

AN OLD CAVE

I headed down the hill and south
into the stubborn crotch of the county

and behind me the sharp string of bluegrass
grew faint as a dead lover's wish,

where I have slept alone for more
years than fingers on my hand, my hand

on the walking stick where I leaned,
and put my weight against the rock, the grub

of animals in the spring, the spring
of water from an overgrown source,

and the music still trickling down to me
from that empty bed, sagging in the middle,

its single oval depression like a cocoon,
like an old cave the neighbors speak of

that I searched for one hot day in August,
and found tucked between two legs of the terrain

that broke apart in a great hairy V.
I messed and pushed my way into

clawing at the dirt, looking for a level
place to step and a view of the meeting place,

the hollow mouth, the lung full of stillness
down where the eyes must invent their own light.

I stood at the old cave
and could hear inside

a depth that makes the body shallow,
a peace like no other

beyond the narrow entrance,
the walls of wet mud.

They say there is a curve
tight as a hidden snake,

that I could never make,
and I shuddered at the thought

that inside, beyond the brave crawl
was space enough to build a house,

grow a tree, take a hand in mine.
I leaned in as far as I could

without venturing into the darkness
that finally took hold and froze me.

I stood in it for years, frightened
that intimacy would find a way to kill me.

I came home through the familiar
green and purple wild-flowers,

and I jumped over the living creek,
my walking stick like a friend

I had made on a playground
when I was ten,

and I continued home,
this place I know like a bird knows air.

I put the walking stick on the porch
and kicked the dirt from my shoes,

opened the white door, came up these stairs,
sat up in bed, sweat trickling down my belly.

The music had stopped,
and a dog was barking at a pair of blue-jays.

NIGHT PASSING

The night is in that special way
blacker than her darkest prime
as all the birds asleep
beneath a cloud of hush,
and the moon, it shines,
a pendant about her neck,
innocent and white again,
over the hill and tree,
the forgotten colors all black,
bark scars of pick and axe.
She is alive and full of age
like the wind lifted roof;
she leaks into the window,
and everywhere she is at ease,
across the desk, a lady in lust,
in the chair, over the bed
curled about herself like a cat,
an eye of black, a wing of bat.
There is no place she will not go,
where there is nothing,
where there is no one;
she is there already in waiting
at a cave undiscovered,
a drawer rusted shut,
in the mouth that never opens,
on the tongue that feels no breath.
She is the one to whom
the moon was promised
and even yet delivered.
There is no diva but her,
no Madonna, no mother
in waiting without her.

She is swollen with everything,
time suckles from her breasts,
the star-light-milk of nipples;
gathering in her belly
the child she raises from darkness,
a spider of gold
that eats its lovely mother
and dies from the guilt.

CURATOR

At night you are a canvas
pulled taught from shore to shore.
A perfect imitation of the moon
laden upon your blue leather
shakes like silk in a breezy window.
Every crest of you which is not city
is the curvature of hidden fish
moving through the bridge's legs.
Lovers are silent by your side
wishing to say to each other
what gentle permanence flows.
The dark island of exploding green
where ducks move like winding toys
around the banks is but a stroke of black.
The relief of fallen driftwood
juts from your ebony chest
like a rib crying out in a dream.
There a silhouette of some avian mystery
alights upon the gravure of sad wood
as the sound of an ocean channeled
hums like a pile of autumn leaves.

MASCARON

My eyes are fish bagged for a dark carnival,
a bazaar along the waterfront where children
can win me with water pistols and plastic darts.
My tongue is a nickel tossed into a fountain.
I am drowning in other people's desires.
My ears are jet engines with no oil, screams.
An odor of fat sweat licks me like intimate rape.
I see my shadow and do not recognize
a strange undiscovered love.
I am a day spent working, not to be remembered.
My cock is a rag for bar spills.
My hands are selling for ten cents at a card-table
yard sale. "Born" is an elegant word.
There is no part of me left.
All my bones have changed like outdated clothes.

CHILDLIKE

Who said when green, a branch holds no fires?
I cannot say it now to make it not awkward
though they are common dreams.
One was to drive a certain car I'd seen
beside a pretty girl on the cover of a magazine,
and then of course to cruise around the city
with the pretty girl, emphasis on *pretty*
and I guess I wanted to hit a baseball
over every parking lot and shopping mall
every school yard and Central Park
and on and on forever into a million hearts.
Melville roams the sea salt yet across the earth
in Pequod's belly. Neruda made love to a million lonely
women, while speaking for a million lonely men.
Dreams are a string pulling loose from the shirt.
So, still this branch burns ever on.
Something awkward will remain in them.
I sense that dreams are always green.

UNEXPECTED

Underneath the fingernails of scarred criminals
are bedded children waiting to be read to sleep.
Someone shuffles with mad eyes shifting in an alley,
for sunshine, for candy whispers to take,
for the doppelganger to come gently by their side,
to say, "Here, here is the ride of a lifetime, hold."
I am troubled enough by the plain blue sky.
The tugboat captain is floating, his girlfriend in the city
sits on an iron landing by the window.
There is a job to be done, a lunch of fruit
settled into the stomach of a captured body.
Libraries of the future must be filled with regal fury,
and the virgin page has never been so white.

KENT,

I guess it is the quiet in the car as you read
that causes me to remember back
before those hands could type.
One August, after I'd stretched out fifteen years
I stole your scooter because you left the key in it
and me and Mark Forman rode
miles into the night clinging to each other like
queers as we giggled and honked the sorry horn
at girls that didn't look up and we rode out past
all the lights of the neighbor's TVs
snubbing the stop signs and stop lights until
there were none, only fields of corn, dangerous curves
power lines running off to greet distant lights
before the descent into the darkness of the hollow
where wise kids said the Devil was worshipped
beside a wall of graffiti and scattered cigarette butts.
We turned around at the crest, unsure if that little
motor would carry us up out of its chilly legend
and we returned home to Mark's house where
you waited mad as the noonday sun for my arrival.
I thought you were going to smash my lip
when you cornered above me in the pressboard kitchen
glaring like a red-hot hammer, eyes cutting me back.
But you didn't. Instead, you shook your shoulders,
dusted the indignity from your chest, and moved on
like a hot pellet in the steamy water of the night.
You didn't talk to me for days but we ran
in the same circles, saw the same faces, we came up
again and you accepted me. How many times have we
fallen into the directions of our own lives, the promise
of jobs, the secrets of faraway classrooms
the cold room (carpeted on the outside) that has no floor

the haunt of our stark families, or the sunshine
in a hand brown as tea against the light? And each
saw our return to some central purpose, a reason
that brought us back and said that we were not finished
with this sophisticated spin, the weave of the common heart
so that it is easy for me to wish all good things for you
and your wife, my gentle friend.
                                      And how funny this moment now
as we ride together for ten hours this gray Sunday
with a metal book of blank pages
we will fill one by one. How funny, that you should ask me,
as you finish and put them on the floorboard,
"What are you going to do with
your poems?" I thought I made that clear years ago.
I'm going to love you with them until we're home.

THE WEIGHT OF BROKEN GLASS

SUNDAY MORNING

The road is quiet
and the streetlamps keep
the moonlight in bay
above the river city
through these windows,
strays upon the sidewalk
searching for a palm of rain,
a midnight wind rolls through Portland.
The open door closes
on its own with a little sigh.
I will lead you as I step
in places I have been alone
and your voice killing shadows
sounding through the cavern
herald to a permanent dawn.
Lover, the house is silent
and it is the calm of a beginning,
which I have never begun
a chance of all the beautiful dreams
still moving with velocity
away from the origin of the sun.
The spacious cradle of dust
where starlight calls home
silent explosions of countless
shades of fire
so far away it is like science fiction,
like a sexual fantasy
made up of partners without faces
without eyes to stare at when we cum.
No name to whisper when we smile.
No ear to catch the jokes we tell.
Breaking down the solitude

of all these homes
and shipwrecked cabins.
How bearable that I should lose a finger
that a phantom there should linger
a spirit to calm the suffering transition
that a part of all of me
torn asunder and ripped to dust
by steel and grease
and two old belts gnawed at the edges
could be made whole
in an evening of your attention.

THE FIRE BELOW

The mess we made since yesterday
has toppled semblance in our room;
the clearings overgrown with weeds
of too much time together,
and pant legs twisted up like snakes
curling through the garden,
rustling the heather planted in the spring.
I wonder if there has ever been
such anger as the one in hand,
filling this giant room,
and filtering out the flue,
topping off the fireplace and mantle?
We covered miles and miles
of dirty city with our love,
disturbing the loneliness of bums,
and leaking from the bricklayer's portal
like a smoke carrying with it
the red of its fire down below.

CONTINENTAL SONNET

You have made your continental escape
so far away, a mile for each sweet kiss
we kissed and all our lives now on we'll miss
what would have been the wine from our love's grape.
It seems a shame to let it sit so late
in the bottom of the bottle remiss.
Never to be savored over these lips
from whose kisses the wine comes in its wake.
Because I think in you I learned to love,
I wanted to give this love to you alone
as if the meat from plants you toiled to plant,
but now I find these roots in hand, a grove
that yearns to touch the soil, to sleeve the bone
to drink the wine beside what grows so giant.

ANOTHER

The appearance of red hair floating in water,
and slowly, I am troubled bone, dry rain
tapping the flesh like sub-dermal ants,
and I am fingertips massaging the eye.
A glorious part of you I carve from tree smoke.
If you would but appear like evasive spots
materializing in the darkness of closed lids,
then I could reach gingerly into my house
and take you from the planter like a flower.
What of green light leavens in this sad story?
My neighborhood morning, my leather chair?
Yet, there will never be another to clash,
to lift, to riot out the tender cafés of me.
If my longing for your once-young neck
were currency, I could buy all the boats
which float in the hot and yellow Kentucky.
If the seconds of this army of recollection
were messages of love and loneliness,
perhaps another would come along
and slide onto me until you were forgotten.

THE LOVER

I gaze through an old photograph of a window
into the haunt of my early twenties to find you

and notice you have stepped from the white edges,
gone since we last touched full in 1992.

This picture of the living cloth you wore.
You lay beyond this separation and so two years ago

I climbed the elm in my back yard and took down
the rope that threatened to take my life.

And later that night I collapsed into a heap
of self-forgiveness, and I cried in the shower

until I couldn't stand, and I sat down naked
full of hope and fear, shaking for an hour

as the water ran against the porcelain,
circled clockwise down the silver drain.

There was no doubt you were my only lover,
that I heard your love over the rain.

But I pushed you away, made you love me more,
climbed on top of you in every position

even invented some of my own and I still pushed away,
made you love me even more until your heart's swell

I broke with the finger used to stroke your nipple hard.
This ugly dance where one is always left in fire.

APHONIA

There are some things
a man learns not to say
because the saying
(he has learned)
changes none of the essence
of his unsaid thing.
So, the silence, then,
becomes what changes,
what is articulated around
the eyes perhaps—
in the hands—
wherever the voice retreats to
when it no longer wants
to stretch
like a tortoise head retracted
when it is useless
to explain what will not heal.

AN ACCOUNT OF MY BIRTH

My first memory,
41 years old, is going after
a toy in the yard
       on Willis Avenue
and the concrete steps, each
as high as my little rubbery knees,
between me and the toy
and from the high porch
       falling all the way
down to the concrete approach
at the ground level of
       the world outside.
I cried exactly like a child.

      *

Thirteen years later, I was sixteen
and I could have been in some pain
when I rolled a pickup truck
in a stranger's cornfield
but I do not remember it
       that way.
I remember noise of crushing glass,
tires punching the tilled earth
       violently
like a boat breaking a wave
then stillness and simply
       not being dead.

      *

Once, while stupidly not being
        in the moment
I wandered my left index finger
into a jointer missing its guard
I remember screaming
in a language one cannot spell
and bleeding everywhere
        I went
until the hospital
put an end to all that
and sewed it shut ever since.

      *

I remembering missing out
on love across several years
and that love, green-eyed
and soft skin as white as a page
and red-haired with curves
like a crescent moon
and a smile
I cannot think upon
longer than I can hold my breath;

      *

Imagining love
that waited on you
until it could wait no more:
Neosporin does not
clean the wound.
No professional under oath
assesses the trauma
and pulls it taught over the bone
        to hold it.

Yes, you remember
until you've worn a hole
into the endless pitch-black sky
      of countless stars.
You look for anything
to fill that up.
You fill it up
with Jim Beam, with
      various drugs
and other lost souls
and poems like this
until you realize
the space is endless.

KICKBALLS AND OVERGROWN LAWNS

WINTER

The worst I'd say it ever got,
minus the weekend when I couldn't move
through the avalanche of empty bottles,
was the night I passed out driving home
and woke up in an exploding ditch.
A geometric mile was the only difference
between me and a newspaper headline.
But I got out and walked home,
a long distance through sweet bark and leaf.
There were drinks to be had yet.
Six more years and loneliness like a pet fish.
I lied, something I rarely do, to the tow trucker.
What good is a confession
if it doesn't save a soul?

VIOLENCE

I have a boxer's break in my right hand,
and an upper lip sewn shut, from another scuffle.
And I've felt a man's nose shatter beneath my fist.
And I've kicked a rude fellow in the side of his head
until he no longer moved in the street where we met
outside that closed bar on Baxter Avenue.
And consider the violence of past thoughts,
the righteous gore of fantasy, entrails pulled out
and splashed across the billboard of my soul, announcing:
Here was some nameless hate, killed by a friendly fellow
turned vicious for all who can't bear to look inward
and see what lies empty like a fire-gutted home within.
I carry upon me, like a birthmark—no, a scar, the rotten
remains of so many who have lashed out like dumb animals.
And it is skin-deep and no more, for public viewing
and group discussion and human conjecture of what
        changes a man.
What blooms outward until it breaks apart into dust
and only ideas remain and ghosts and shadows on the ground
that the wind alone might disturb what has long settled?

KICKBALLS AND OVERGROWN LAWNS

Only the most-vile deprivations wake my lust,
or turn my white skin purple.
When I close my eyes,
whores come to my bedside to be slapped,
and hordes of faceless men
degrade them one by one,
my erection standing, wide of eye.
And, no sooner are they gone,
than a goddess alights to her knees
and opens her mouth
to receive the arch of urine from the cherub's stone.
Sometimes it is me on my knees
before me a man so long and beautiful
he is built to be cruel,
or a teacher from junior high in black leather
a riding crop replacing her powdery yellow chalk.
But it is never, never a woman,
who was once a friend, who is a lover,
who smiles as I enter her,
behind the accordion light of the curtain.
It is never this clean nor fawn-eyed dream.
A nurse made this promise to me when I was 12.
A neighbor to a 12-year-old from a two-income home
a man who thought little boys
were for better things than kickball in the street
and mowing lawns for $10, *or did he bargain for $8.50?*
In the context of his desire, he promised me
one of two things as a man:
unconditional love or immense loneliness,
and then a third:
a poem about myself.

SOMETHING THAT HAPPENED BEFORE I THOUGHT OF YOU

Long ago I imagined death,
like a tree imagines itself
in the landscape it does not have
the eyes to see.
I figured I could chase it from my body
if I filled every inch of me
with Kentucky bourbon.
And then it was too late,
it was belly fat
and dropout soup.
It was six, eight years underwater.
When I saw what was happening
and came up and surprised
even myself, drawing an awesome breath
so that I did not look back,
(somehow always knowing
which way just was *back*).
Until today, for some reason
today I looked back.
It was very clever,
what death had done,
and I cried when I realized.
I cried and then I screamed,
and I hugged myself,
and I thought of you.
I must have looked like an idiot,
but you would have understood.
It would have made you believe
in a damned good God.
I can't wait to see you next
and hold you.

SOBER

Over the steel suspension of the bridge
I see fragments of what came apart,
screaming yet in car horns,
the watery scent of spun wind,
the brush which grows by moonlight even.
It is not all bad.
Here goes the river
between these two cities,
spilling into the larger body
of the cold ocean.
Yet the river
does not need to see its way,
it needs no illumination.
This dark night—
years ago,
all things, all of my bones
were pressed smaller
than that which expresses now.
Light suppressed inside
an empty fist.
Where have I returned?
This homecoming?
But, look out there,
the light is but a dust
in the vast darkness
that once could not get in.

EVERYWHERE, SOMETHING

for myself

You said you wanted nothing for Christmas
but that you cannot have.
Everywhere I look, a branch in ice,
a breath like compost steam,
where the birds deserted the wire roads,
it is something. Everywhere, something.
In the porous afterglow of your taillights,
in a bleak silence that spills seconds out between us,
in my failures as a man, in the blasted white moon,
my mind rushes in and fills up the voids like a voice fills a hall.
I have learned to forgive myself
what I cannot control.
Now in my hands, there is patience,
a mortality, so tender as to be infinitely beautiful,
a ring around your waist,
and I cannot give you nothing
any more than the ice can be chipped away
and the road hammered until there is no earth.
What I give is being given even now
silent, invisible as they say.

BLACK HARVEST

What was once a pitcher's arm,
a writer's hand,
a biker's foot, all
carried off in the vacuum,
pieces of yesterday's forest floating slowly away,
white sawdust in the emptied shop,
ghosts who rise before me,
climbing toward the nearest light.
I am no longer just the trunk of a torso,
a growl in the throat, a brain sharp as shark's teeth—
madness threatens as
thick as a cotton blanket.
I watch for a sign, maybe two spoons of sugar
for the day-old coffee.
I'd settle down, give thanks,
if the trees out this window
all turned on humanity,
and they morphed
into 50-foot-tall butterflies,
and they ripped apart the beautifully crafted yards
to free the roots of their crepuscular legs,
and they took flight into the cloudy sky
until the sun was blocked,
and there was nothing but the sound of flapping,
great flags of swirling colors
to redefine the universe.
I would feel sorry for no one.

ON VALUE

I predict that the impact of my coming and going
will never fully be known, and that in all estimations

the enterprise of this humble venture into the common
market, the value of this view from my green window,

the degraded nostalgia of the stars,
the village of weeds by the corner stone;

the simplest things are meaningless,
the bough of the thick tree can break and fall

without consequence and deteriorate into muck;
complexities do not move us in fascination,

and the road in its own time and place—
that is country and leaf, that is wild dog and stray cat,

that is the hill-top to the south looking a thousand feet
down into the city, the soiled city, the frolicked city;

the people in their lives and their careers, their tags,
their fashions, and their styles of cars, they too must know,

must understate it always, the meaning of their lives.
For to say that the horse-fly, whose bite is like a driven nail,

has significance or to find pleasure in the water-man
who is bitter as stale wine when he visits to fill my cistern;

then, what miseries must we get bogged down in,
or what beauty must happen to change our minds?

I'VE BECOME THE RIVER

The river's birth is a free fall
from the sky,
an explosion from the soil
into a canal
cradled in the continent
that would have it so.
Then the path is taken
overland, through the low places
underground, where it finds a space
around the immovable.
So, the corners are formed
the jettisoned angles
where the water fishtails
caroms from the bank
and pulls itself forward
once again.
For centuries the river cut
ruthlessly, adamantly
determined to straighten
the route of its eternal journey.
The river is always beautiful,
always lush and contorted,
always working to carve its perfect trail.
In a world where being hard
is precious,
where the very meaning of strength
is to never give way,
the river seems to yield
at every obstacle.
Yet, once seeming
it proceeds to spill
into what lies beyond.
All the world
a decorum on its banks.

THE DANCE OF THE BLACK WASPS

TOO LATE, THE WINDY EVENING HAS COME

There are inhumanities which grow upon us
like leaves, nameless and green,
beneath the sunlit noon of days
until they cover us in their shade.
For some time, I marveled at their beauty,
the sheer growth of what I had not known
the day before, in the childish minutes
of my bucolic terrain, my sweet pasture.
These leaves, grown by moonlight even,
stay and steal away to ever darker hues,
until you see them for what they are
and all is lost. You cannot dismiss
yourself, what grows upon you, with a
"Go home! I do not want you anymore!"
They curl back from the serrulate cusp,
and wrap their cells like a throat
around the veins that bore them.
They engulf the bones like desiccate flesh,
like the ever sunken and soiled roots.
The roots forever in darkness, always,
and the leaves, left to shudder in the wind.

EVOLUTION

I've seen too many crushed upon the road.
The slop of their insides spilled beneath
their crustaceous backs like radiated beetles
exterminated by the stomp of disgusted giants.
But they do not hide by the hundred-thousands
in the toaster shadows, the kick of the cabinets.
They do not fester in weary places of the home
and infest the somnambulant bacterial splash.
They march slowly through the pink-haired fields,
alone, their abbreviated elephant legs swimming
toward some greater shell of prehistoric caul.
Their hawk's head, their lizard's neck
brushing aside the towers of spider grass
like a careful gamer moving slowly his queen.
Then, before them like a river before
a rider and his horse, this belly of stone
humming with some latent energy come
from above or below his vegetative plane.
I've seen too many crushed upon the road
and I've seen the future of the tortoise.
His hate-black heart lined with explosives
and the front end of some ignorant hick's
jacked Monte Carlo flying into deadly pieces
above the wet-weather ditch like flak
in a melee pitched over civilization's fate.

RADIO TOWER

In the construction paper black of night
a blinking light atop a tower of steel
warns drunk pilots and myopic birds.

White as a camera flash it sends
a pulse over the hill like rain-walls crashing
into their selves upon the swollen ground.

Not quite every second it flits across ten thousand
faces of leaves and spines of grass
aluminum fence-gates and backyard windows.

It spills up into the sky like a scream
dulls the brilliant moon and smears the stars
with small images of itself stained upon the eyes.

Looking to its bulb in the closed-bag dark
of an approaching storm it shrieks from its perch
and no two splashes of white are just alike.

It is electric snow, an eternal flame honoring
a dead hill worshipped by confused deer
who look up and whisper a neologism in doe-tongue.

The soft pink leather lips say: it is a shaft fallen from deep
       in the soil
into the sky during a moment when gravity went haywire
and we ourselves could not jump a common fence.

That light, an eyeball of the earth's hidden flame
was snagged by the shaft as it raced into the atmosphere
until the great legs of creek stone, gray as water-sanded shale,

came to a rigid halt and the molten pool risen to meet the air
cooled into a cube at its feet until its grip
was as a youth who tries to keep some loved life from the dead.

What was unexplained by this new and frightful word
they bleated alongside the dry creek beds of the low places
was the constant blinking of the terrestrial beacon

as if it were struggling to say something it could not.
Chewing on the grass reflected in those anthracite eyes,
tuned to the wind, the deer make no sound.

THE RUN OF THE SQUIRREL

A squirrel is a small thing in the world.
The one from yesterday was gray as cinder
and nervous eyes black as coal
hidden in a closeted box.
He stood on hind legs like a fat-bottom woman.
His hands dangling and empty
and then he sprang at the sound
of my predacious steps.
Dexterous fingers dug into the scaly bark
and lifted him, a flashing tail, into the sun.
Like a banded barber's pole he turned
about in his ascension
his little meaning, until
he breached the lower branches.
He spread out: a bloom, a hunter
of shelled organs, a feral rat,
straining my neck to see him go along.
He ferried the aggregate limbs,
danced like music, and called my name
in a foreign language; some warning.
Then he scuttled to the waxen tapered end
of a newest growth.
Here he found a train at the final station.
A man at peace killing time.
Blood in the vessel's end
as fine as a dying star.
An arm's stretch of yarn.
A leap into the air
or an art.

TABLE PRAYER

There are words to represent our
own particular fascinations, to suggest
the wonderment we find with that
singular view called the personal.
There are words to entomb a sole
understanding, to celebrate anomalies,
and to call forth the brilliant passages
that befall each of us, in our turn,
in private retreats of place of time.
There are words in our hands to hold
meaning, to imply what suffering
we have endured to deserve now this;
these dark and wonderful words
that there are enough of for each
to take some, to pull from pockets
in times of hunger, to dust in old age;
words to fill the plates we sit in front of,
where our reflections stare back at us.

CICADA

This is not a poem about cicadas.
Not about their seventeen-year gestation
nor the collective whirl of sound
surrounding the embedded listener
as if a 1960s Hollywood flying saucer
were landing in the bald knoll
of the forest where they've awoken.
This is not about the hundreds
of thousands of them clinging
to the thin wisps of lily reeds
nor the finger-nail translucent
husks of themselves left over
like a chrysalis self-portrait.
This is not a verse about the .22 caliber
holes in the mud floor of the woods
from which they crawled
like damned things arisen
to a tactile afterlife, a hardened ghost hood
of mindless parasitical coming.
This evasive subject does not take flight
nor rest throughout a generation.
It is few, indeed, it is but one
here-and-there and it does not cry-out
in special effect or sculpt itself
in delicacies the wind can disturb.
And it does not turn up from the soil
but rather sinks into it like a farmer's hand
and stays like a thirsty root.

AUTUMNAL

Puddled in the husks of themselves
they happen from the saturated mud
like an opened eye delivers
the vision kept in wait.
They are startled by the sun,
crushed into a thousand directions
though they are following but one.
Here, the wind takes a shape,
the rain grows a skin,
and the weight of light breaks all rock.
Green is the first color
one might call colorful,
its pinched between the finest fingers
at the ends of giant arms, waiting.
Then, suckled from the depths
and carried in the veins,
these pastel inclinations ferried into
the reason, the very meaning
of the seed's ancient sewing.
Soon enough, this rustiness settles over
the vast changeling of the canopy
and the reds are less so,
the oranges and the yellows...
until the sere shells hang
like skeletons on a rope
and then they fall
to rejoin the roots.

OHIO RIVER

Without the river, islands are merely hills,
and birds journeying to the islands are approachable.
I prefer that some fish, some birds be out of reach.
It is good to know that some alluvial dweller
can slip into her dress of darkness and be gone
like a child swallowed up in raked piles of leaves.
One day this river will rise up from the earth
in science fiction, in glasslike form,
and we shall see the glory of her skeleton
floating into the space of love-filled minds.
Because the river is a saint, she nurtures
the poorest among us; they sit under bridges
and watch her stroll along; they own her
as much as the captain of the smartest yacht.

THE NIGHT RAIN

How quickly the night rain turns the river lonely.
The clouds move into view like a chemical
burning out the stars, searing the moon
into a milky spill that bleeds across heart-broken miles.
The lovers all at once drop each other's delicacies
and turn for the warm acres of dark dry automobiles.
Birds which floated through the lemon light
of rustic wharf lamps disappear like hunted treasures
to clandestine perches built in the cleft of angle irons
running through the distant cats-cradle bridges.
The once flat finish of the waterfront pavement
turns glossy and coins of rainbows affix themselves
to the atoms of drizzle the stubborn headlights pierce.
Even the smells are subdued, the green odor
of afternoon mowing along the muscle of concrete.
The hot light scent of oil where battered cod
fries in the neon fish house. The perfume of the lady
patrons are all washed into the dancing black water.
Weekend sailors warm their palms on coffee.
Rubber fishermen reel in empty lines
from the cryptic barbed hooks, they see
the ugly faces of their wives, hear them in the thunder
leave them on the ice of the beer cooler.
Only the fish are charmed and congenial.
They fly into the air like acrobats.
Their gills fold out like lawn chairs, becoming wings.
Supernatural and wall-eyed, they explode
into drenched upright monsters.

PRAYER

It is true the body falls apart.
It exhales slowly some great magic,
and all at once, like an army suddenly on a hill,
we realize that which does not crumble
beneath the house like too much rain.
So, what of the spirit?
Is it overrated, overwrought with charlatans?
Who, even in their estimation,
seem to know, too, of the valley
lost beyond this cracked city
where the heart which piloted blind
this body, this carrier of lust and dream,
dwells and does not know a sour grape,
but rather breaks over and over again,
like water on green precious stones,
and simply gathers again
in pool, in greater hopes,
shapes of ancient low settled things.

TOAD AS ORPHAN

Like I myself one day
came into this house alone,
a toad of leathery brown
and salted green creeps
hunched and neckless
through the white door.
Full of a silent instinct,
a swollen throat, a sore
and weary eye and
of all the creatures
wandered from the forest—
cooed by the warmth
and the smell of living air;
the dank joint of earth and brick;
the oven crumbs and
closed drawers of cotton—
I leave only him to be in peace
among the blood-filled paper-waste
and the sound of feet
on hollow wood and piled stone.
While these miracles the rest hunt
among the field and walls,
the pillars of brick and towers of ash;
the fox, the snake, the coon,
the turkey, the spider, and the hawk,
stepping, high-kneed and straight back
through the porch, among the jamb and plate
over my darkened shoulder
where the night has drawn its black cape—
these, they engulf us.
For each they run, or fly, or build your web
where you hang in brilliant suspension.

DRAGONS

Loch Ness is said to lurk
in the evening of our fears,
like the family cat I hardly see
leaping black from the pine porch
galloping across the chalk
behind the fading tree
into the gothic pond, the sea.
Rumors hardly do a justice
to a hunted thing
who yellow-eyed and snarling
wisps across centuries
like a mouse behind a curtain,
snake-tailed and still
living between our curiosities.
Gigantopithecus, ornery and free
loping in the fly-over
with shoulders wide as northwest
valleys, who came once across
the Bering Strait in snow prints,
following the myths of ancestors,
talk of lassitude imbued mammoths
wild boars lumbering in never ending
circles made of circles.
So, what of Dragons?
Men in antelope fur
found million-year-old bones
wide as the mouths of caves
and what majesty like this,
what divine scale of femur and rib,
would be delivered mundane, un-winged?
Reports were made of a tongue-and-flame
like water from a spring.

Many minds were crippled, armored bodies killed
while naked men squared to the unseen—
these the fire cleaned.

THE SINGING OF THE WASPS

These wasps we watch gather
at the roof of the porch,
come each spring like invited dignitaries,
like the budding poplar leaves
        of green.
In more anxious brattier days,
blind to what they gave,
one by one with my right-handed club,
I killed them, fearful of their sting.

These wasps we watch gather
at the roof of the porch
are busy, always busy, with their work.
Yet no tedium, I can grasp, hangs
heavy from the black vests.

These wasps we watch gather
at the roof of the porch
are sure about what they do,
and being older now,
and closer to my doubt,
I let them live, like a soothing melody
painted blue.

AVALANCHE

> *"The best life never leaves your lungs."*
> —*Jeff Tweedy*

The earth is pliable at best,
molten statuaries feeding
the ballast taking us around
the sun we serve as moon.
Ancient biospheres go under,
melt to gold, burn, buoy
the concretized chrysalis.
Constant awakenings like these
shake the body for miles deep
and in the end, (if it be called),
they reverberate in salty oceans
promulgate waves that tackle boats
and reshape pristine shorelines
or a mountain drops its face.
With an avalanche, the air
out front gets you first.
It leaves you breathless
when these shifts occur
without a feeble notion.
Then the snow, then the snow
settling below where feet
will pack it in, burn trails.
Above, inexplicable curves
once hidden, turned to the sun,
cold and glorious, beckoning.

KIND EULOGY

We cannot see our lives buried.
The grit brown coming up like water.
The dream houses sinking, broken hulls
roads to trails to paths to flyover tracts
of spilled nature, crocus and dandelion
where leashed dogs once sniffed
and elk munch over shipwrecked swag
fifty thousand years deep into her.
Once so often I am beset with a fear
I cannot describe to convey the inside.
The germination is when people say of a piece
"What is it about?" It is about a color,
you can only look at its every word together
to know, is to speak the language
or to breath, to thank the sun before going.

A week ago, they found a coyote
wandered from outer space and cornered
in a parking garage next to the tall building.
When they came for it with nets and poles
I saw my teeth fall out in a horrible dream.
It's beautiful fatal eyes, the palpitation in
the tongue while it danced feral on the stone.
They took him to a refuge in a far county
the way we see to it that the dead also go.
But they are such good friends, silent
in the know and keeping secrets
greater than the waiting in our minds.

LIKE TREES LIKE WATER

Like trees like water
there is a viscosity
in all the greenery.
It moves too slow
for human interval
but comes true
to form nonetheless.
A seed breaks its bulb
like an explosion
in outer-space
it is pre-dawn quiet
without fire.
Then a rib floats up
from last year's top soil
lifting the weight
of an angel's thinking.
Sunlight's melody
starts the garden dancing.
A crowd is on their feet.
The whole world changes
in a single bloom.

RED

It seems but a style for roses and lips
or a thread sewn into chintz.
Yet we imagine our hearts are filled with it
like the burning end of a cigarette.
Ginseng beads and cherry trees
fire ants and certain maple leaves
have taken from the spectrum
that first of seven decorum.
Broken flesh reveals it
caustic thick and wet
and the virgin legs conceal it
like a veil from a coronet.
In Nature it is danger
as in emotion it is anger.
In the sunset it is beauty
like a ribbon on the sea.
It cracks the white of tired eyes
writing poems 'til sunrise.
Makes its way into fountain pens
velvet cake and chrysanthemum.
It is Mars and dye in a teenager's hair
holding the galaxy together.

MIDNIGHT PRAYER

There is a road to bring me here,
and glaciers that melt each summer,
like the glaciers melting in us,
and they stand above the tree line
where nothing grows and speak of cold.
When warming, water runs down
the mountain, puddling in mud,
and eventually, me standing in this
snow, a naked man on white paper.
It fills a lake-bed passed by yawning
tourists and indentured by the locals.

I feel a chill at midnight and wonder
who has felt it before.
There is a road to take me out of here,
but I feel a chill and I do not know if
the mountain feels it too.
The sun will rise and warm its tired crown.
Perhaps the light will clothe me.

THE DANCE OF THE BLACK WASPS

First, the moon was full and white as a clean skull
beyond the arch of branches off the trunk
and what I thought was a single distant owl
full of grace among the August air, the summer leaves

flew directly at me, probing this side
of the window, throwing shadows off the candle
and came to be a wasp against the only light
black as burnt glass, long as a facial scar.

I turned and shook my head, to lose
its sudden rage in vain, its trip across the sky
dragging yellow fire like a comet, speaking
a language as direct as touch.

It dipped and turned in frenzies
and was lost against the shadows of the rafters
then came into view again, wings buzzing
like a page of a book caught in a violent wind.

Then a second came from the night
eight legs dangling in the space of my room
like a descending spider's
weaving themselves into the lottery of my blood.

A third and then a fourth, a troupe of them
in moments, about my head like a crown
my feral dodge, this leap against the letting go
and the mass of them tethered to my memory,

satellites in orbit about the earth,
moving in a space in which the end cannot be

imagined, this room where they crowded in commune
one night equaling myself, eclipsing, yet again,
                                        the moon.

NO BOTTOM

THE STATE FAIR

I wandered away from those simple rides
and my mother's hand sat empty
for a moment useless among the crowd
and beat a path to Madame Fortuna's
red drape of a tent and the folded darkness
where she sat at that table-clothed
card table on an old wooden chair
telling round-eyed children of their dreams
and calling forth visions of our adulthoods.

I saw her peering into a little girl's forehead
her dark painted eyelids pulled back
from her big blue and red eyeballs
that shot like hot pokers into the cold air
of that child's future and the little girl's
mother stood by patiently waiting to hear
that she was raising a Natural,
a child of promise and reward
to make the family proud of their daughter's mother.

Madame Fortuna scowled from time
to time and then she told the two,
"You will grow up to be a beautiful woman,
not like your mother. So, learn to cry tears
so soft they don't even strike the floor.
Do this whenever things are going wrong
and it will fix everything, your tears."
The angry mother took her daughter
away from the mouth of the tent.

When I stepped from the draped shadows
into the light of candles, of classrooms,

of empty aisles and morning lit bedrooms
she saw me and my kind and took me
to her table and I knew my chair
across from her and that pool of vision
where she cast her ringed fingers
and the bracelets on her thick wrists
jangled in the heavy air of her jobbing.

"What about Mother and Father?"
I asked not knowing any better, scared
even to be away from them
but Madame Fortuna had seen me before
and she warned me that it was bigger than that
and her words shut me down like a light
she peered into and I became hollow again,
the colors of the room shining through me
until my mother could not find me among the noise.

"Never mind that, child, you are growing
incredibly fast, fast as weeds after a rain storm
and it's a big state fair out there, ripe for being lost.
You're hardly even the same boy that walked in
here but the worst of it is yet to come. There's
a pain like eating bees that you can't spit out.
How old are you child? Ten, you say. Well
it couldn't be worse than that. There's never been
a worse time to be a poor white ten-year-old boy."

"But I'm fast as a baseball. Strong as a bat.
And I'm not afraid to punch the bullies
in the courtyard at lunch. I'm smarter than
the nerds and I've got more rhythm than the band,"
I said to her, angry that my mouth was full of stingers.
"Shut up, that doesn't matter a day's pay kid.
Look at you popping out of your britches.

The books are slipping from your arms into puddles.
Remember when you and your brothers were the same?"

"I'm made of long wet roots and soy milk.
I'm loved like the Lord loves an animal.
In my soul is the beginning of jazz and
the lines of great buildings in the clouds.
I've been inspected by angels and blinded
by stars I've counted from my dreams to sleep.
Can't I share this and then things would be different?
The people waiting at the entrance could come in."

"Each will come in turn, now is yours
and now I see. You talk like a man already.
So, I can tell you that it will happen
earlier rather than later and there is
nothing you can do about it. It can't be stopped.
Sometime when you are standing, minding
your own business, someone will walk by
your shoulder and from behind, as you count
your money, someone will smack you hard and solid

in the side of your face. Centuries of the dead
will witness your indignity and confusion
as the stranger that struck you for no reason
disappears into the dining room full of other strangers.
You will get a glance of the back of his head
before you realize your mistake and blame yourself."
She folded her arms in silence as I kicked the leg
nervously waiting for her to finish with a story
like Saturday morning cartoons.

But she said nothing else and I pushed my big knees
away from that flimsy scam and wandered out
among the reality and miracle of the afternoon.

Suddenly, in the noise of the crowd, my pocket
ripped open and all my game change rolled down
my leg and into the hurried feet of the celebrants.
I was thrashed about as I dove for the hopeful well,
looking for the bright disks barely seen
and lost among the shadows.

ON THE RADIO AFTER THE STORM

I

Bluegrass music makes me happy
like the unsold seed grown wild
like a rope of lightning
or the sound of a tree falling
to the corrosion of wind-punch.

II

The young men, all fed, came home.
Two trees lay in the yard.
Two days' work sometime soon.
The incidental sound a long time gone.
The green-eyed one turned from pudding
        visions...
"I would like to have been here,
you know. I'm sure it was a hell
of a boom. Still, it's nice some things
can't be controlled."

THE MCALPINE LOCKS

The diver squared the tank upon his shoulders
and fixed the mask about his face
and leaped from the wall to the water
where he broke the surface like any other fish.
Construction was finished but a day.
The test run to move a million gallons
had been completed a little after noon
but some anomaly in the movement
left the engineers concerned in the control room.
The diver suited up as he had done a hundred times
and the engineers turned the switch
that cut the power to the turbines
and then he went into the shadows
leaving bubbles in his wake
and he slithered deeper and deeper
his eyes following the light
from his underwater lamp
that showed the turbulence of the current
and the eerie barrier of concrete like Broadway
running through Atlantis after curfew.
As he descended he reached out his free hand
touched the mass of their construction
and went into the depths of the damn
foot-by-flapping-foot and head first
until the pressure popped his ears,
a condition of visitors to the alien atmosphere.
In the murky spew and loam
some greater edifice rested
than that which he followed down
and the light was cut short
where the river met the ground.
Here he turned about and his flippers kicked mud

that rose the same as dirt in a desiccated field
and he must have looked some fire-handed demon
one great big glass eye for a head
and smoke rising up around his torso
conducive to the message he had brought.
Suddenly, from the panoply of shadows
a catfish the size of a canoe
his whiskers thick as a climbing rope
his gills sending a current all their own
seemed startled to find the diver there
and even more so to hit the wall of stone.
As fast as he could manage
he returned home, kicking with all his might
a cloud of white water chased him
and when he told the story later
all the catfish believed and none have returned yet.

NO BOTTOM

The carpenter built his house in Shipping Port in 1922
with his very own hands and he and Peggy Lou
lived there without much worry but what the soil gave
and whether or not the dear would stave
in the fences around the garden's plot of land
and he raised a house, a barn, a five-acre fence by hand
and two children before The Great Depression
turned the tide against a third conception.
The youngest one was eight, the oldest eleven
when that valley rain began to fall in 1937.
Now he had lived along its bank for each of forty-seven years
but could not swim and so the river was all he ever feared.
Going on that second gray day of heavy rain
it seemed the storm had been unchained.
The sky was something altogether other than
what the sky had always been
and when the corner turned on hour forty-eight
and still the wet wind did not abate
the river swell crawled out its bed
like a black snake grown from the skin it shed
crawling without feet, without hands
up the alluvial muck into the fertile lands.
And when the third sun rose behind the ubiquitous clouds
the weak light which fell upon the neighbor's cows
showed the river, too, to be up to their knees
and everywhere a wild thing roosting in the trees.
So, for the first time in his life he set foot into her chill
straight from bed into the current nigh up to the sill
his wife's hand in his, they gathered up the boys
from their little room full of floating toys
and the four followed by the swimming dog
made for the pole barn through the morning fog

where the loft was sure to loom over the water mark
and they must have looked headed for the Ark
when the carpenter filled their arms
with tools to carry to the barn.
"This'll be what we'll need most after she's done,"
was all he said to his wife and to his sons.
And they rose dripping from her current onto the ladder
and he had never seen Peggy's eyes look any sadder
than when her wardrobe came from the front door
and headed for the distant Indiana shore.
They sat there drying off in the extant hay
of the second floor of the barn on the fourth day
and had not noticed the water for some time
until it lapped against the 2x10 a crest of river slime
and the youngest boy cried out and startled all the rest
who rose to their feet and drew a cross about their chest
and said there a quickened prayer which was answered in its kind.
The carpenter drew out a hand-saw like a thought drawn
       from his mind
and set to cutting up the roof which ran over head
and one by one he felled the planks without so much as rested.
When he judged the lumber pile enough to hold their mass
he set about conjoining them into a river flat.
And when the river rose from that barn roof hole
a family burst through like a body giving up a soul
and the father with one long beam in hand
like some mad gondolier did stand
upon the edge of his greatest fear
calling out through the rain and tears,
the depths which his sorrow would contain,
"Quarter less twain! Mark twain! Half twain!"
Until house, barn, and tools were forgotten
and all in vain, he muttered "No bottom."

DISTORTED HISTORY

THE DAY I STOPPED WRITING

In 1942, my grandfather flew home on leave
from Pearl Harbor to an emptied home in San Francisco.

His wife, my grandmother, a long-legged brunette,
who liked operas and department store jewelry,

placed my mother in an orphanage with her brother,
who was born while grandfather flew into a history book.

His sweet bird drifted off to Utah
to chase those dreams of love, that hope of being envied,

that glorious moment when we want for nothing and
    remember forever.
She had the look of captured sunlight, the center of the
    room in her eye,

the elegance of old photos that men would tame, if they could—
and two more tried, giving her each time a child like a bell,

twice again she left them. All of those tomorrows,
four lives worth of sunrise and moonset,

given to the care of strangers, bagged up as cauliflower,
scallops, onions, handed over weeping like April mist.

That first day I came home, shunned by my only love,
I thought of grandfather, the opening of his dry-hinged
    apartment door,

him walking through the hardwood hallway, expectant,
his footprints in the dust, turning corners,

leaving rooms of familiar shapes with nothing,
nothing to refurbish his pre-war hopes,

nothing but the light of the window behind him,
his shadow ahead that seemed to move before he, himself,
    moved.

UNDERMINING

for my father

I woke early:
the way you like to do things.

Cut the cold hard winter
with a borrowed shovel.

Turned over the cat,
balanced her the on the steel palm,

tipped blade in the Earth's favor,
and laid her four legs to rest.

Beside me was the dog
I never had as a child.

And when the silent work was done,
I threw on bundles of clothing,

took him down into the steep
cut of the cold hills.

I grabbed trees to sturdy
the descent, watched him run ahead.

Bounding from withered leaf to fern,
down past the earliest growth.

I fell behind from touching bark,
untangling my feet from roots.

Until that which was leaving me was so far
ahead I'd forgotten its name.

I moved slow and cautious.
I thanked each sprout that marked my way.

Father, I'm lost and fallen from your loins
if you were ever found;

I think that the poplars were forgotten,
the silver-grass cut too soon.

I know you've disapproved of my discoveries,
and the way they came without invoice.

But I'm moving still deeper into the old cracks,
looking for the way back to a place I've never been,

Moving forward in a top-heavy-step,
yelling at the top of my lungs,

"Dusk! Dusk!"
The air ringing from the trees.

I know to celebrate,
even though it might not come back.

Don't you see? I'm undermining
time and space,

chiseling through the poison
we have drunk,

carving out that old-time river
that has but one bank.

Because just up there,
when I buried that shrunken cat

that I had to put to sleep,
because her lungs were filling with water,

I uncovered a dangerous secret.
It squirmed like a shiny worm

in the dull broken mud,
                              then went down.

Jesus Dad, speak with me! The two of us
opening together in the Future's hands.

For all deaths are sudden
and quickly beyond our reach.

THE MEANING OF WORK

There's my mother.
Her hair gray-streaked-brown and curled
as frosted October maple leaves
hanging over denim coveralls
chewing gum discreetly.
She sits at her table
and picks up the menu
my co-worker handed her.
Her elbows land on the laminate
I wiped minutes ago
behind a couple of gregarious lawyers
plotting all the way back to Maine.

My mother orders her food
pulls a romance novel
from her pocket
as I respectfully gather
dirty rounds from 64
and then wipe away the proof
that anyone at all ever cared to visit
this little corner.

The lawyers walk past her
as she turns a page
and I stop beside the pitchers
of soft brown tea and iced water
to check the line of tables
the sunlight falls across
and her face is lit like new copper.

She has come from her own
bosses, her own messes to clean
up behind her lawyers,
men in suits and slick bald heads
that talk of frustrated deals
with casual self-importance
between bites of pesto capellini
and the garlic loaf
tucked onto the edge
of their plates.

My mother bites from hers,
the steam from the broccoli
fills her glasses, she turns
a page as I step quick
to a baby's spill that
runs into his mother's lap.
I can see her hands
as she cleans the crust
from my nose on winter days
so long ago.

Those hands that hold that book.
I know so little of them,
their white knuckles,
their imprinted ends,
the painted teeth, trimmed and
shaved, and the motor
that runs them. I know
that they raised three kids.
Went to community college at night
after ten-hour days, six days a week.
Washed the dirty knees
of my father's duty.
Kept the same job, same marriage

for thirty-five years
and moved into the pressed
skirts and pantyhose, the silent
rules of that place so grim and
full of echo, like a library
without books.

She woke cold winter mornings
to greet the bus
and when it took her there
she would shake her tired eyes open
for that final stop,
crumbs of a hurried breakfast in her lap.
She painted the walls of cheap
apartments she would leave during the
summers in the hands of baby-sitters
referenced from a corkboard
notice hung in the copy room
beside the Pepsi machine.

She took her lunch
in brown bags, drove cheap cars
to put each sprout through college
and made sure that my father
always had a home-cooked meal,
a twelve pack, and a Louis L'Amour novel.
And when the day's drone grew weak
she'd drag herself home to that cheap
apartment, that rented tri-level, that Bedford Stone
to three children that would grope
for her attention, ignorant fingers
pinching her breasts and a husband
that wouldn't answer questions
if he was in between a gunfight
at the Old Saloon

and a wagon chase where one
good white man saves himself
and a batch of peaceful Indians.

This handsome woman,
her red-mock turtle beneath the denim,
whose wrinkles are wrinkles of
times she found to laugh and smile
beneath all the "Huns" and "Babys" in
the file drawer of her curvaceous memory
her mind so irrefutably fertile
although she does not read poetry
she reads cheap romance novels.
Indeed, she reads my poetry.
Reads my heart.
Never raises a voice to my shortcomings.
Encourages me.
Changed my shit-filled diaper.
Made me French Breakfast Puffs.
Bought me books.
Took me to King's Island.
Signed me up for baseball.
Rescued me from jail.

All while she maintained
that daily routine she nailed so well
she was able to balance the scales
of income in our house
with one hand while she
cleaned the glass ceiling with another.
There's my mother.
Her plate cleaned and mopped.
Her book closed.
A mirror in her hand
to properly straighten her lips

with a tiny pencil.
Me, with my bus tub, across the way,
watching her end her lunch hour.
She will return to that place that raised me and
I will be left behind
to my own work. Sorting through
the wet clump of napkins,
the half-eaten chicken, the spilled ice,
the ripped foil packages of dressing.

A SONG FOR MARCIA ON MOTHER'S DAY

In the way that animals we love more than others
seem more human, you have made me a person.
And on this Sunday, we have set aside for healing
the pain of birth, I want a song to fill the air in your name.
Of all that I carry with me in this sheath of leather
that makes me weak or crippled with shame
you are the ballast which has kept me here
in the field of green so lovely water has made its way
and trees have built homes they share with squirrels
who steal pieces of the sun to build nests of gold and green.
So, let the clouds be white today and swim in a pool of blue
notes harmonizing this meal of time, we will spend together.
Let the lyric send our thanks and fill your loving ears and
the wind to lift your soul in a peace you dream of nightly.
Let the food be served to my brothers first and my sisters
and nephews and nieces and to you mother, for I have only
just sat down and my plate is full with your company.
My ears are happy with the sound of your voice
your innocent eyes and your wild gray hair.
You are a matriarch inside the tongue
of the meadowlark set free at birth
to roam among the verdant plush
the routed woods along the tempestuous bank
the step of the sunlight through the timber
and you have given me an eternal song I try to return
in these words, much too heavy to call music, nonetheless.

THE POOR ADDITION

Father, I have my good days
as you had yours as a young man
and as I undo this poor addition
to my house to make way
for something new, I am scared.

The sun reminds me of the hospital
where you took your fill of broken bones
over the years I hardly noticed
so that they could put the glue in you
always returning functional, the family man.

Come from steep hills, you
and seven siblings beneath a tin roof
I slept beneath one camping trip
and I remember thinking that
I would rather have a tent.

And I learned when you were my age,
at the time, water was in rivers and little else
and heat was in the chopped wood
nothing stood still for you and nature
itself came up from the floor.

Father, I know that at sixty-five your bones
remember that your blood was never
thick enough to heat the cracks of that humble home
but you talk of your father as a hero
who lost his right thumb in a hunting accident.

And you tell me that he read you all poetry
and I imagine that after he blew out the light
he kissed you and you remembered it until the morning
when my grandmother would pull you into the honeycomb
of her arms and I hate you for that story.

As I remove the homemade wood paneling of this
goddamned addition I remember that shack you
took us to in Tejas at the hills of the Appalachians
and I shot my great Uncle's 22. caliber rifle at Pepsi cans
my brothers and I had emptied over a long lunch.

Later we hiked in the woods and we found
one of those old creeks that you must have spoken of
because I knew what they meant
but I can't remember you
actually, saying anything to me.

I remember that mother had a hard time
with the angle at some passages
and that Dan and I raced
and Steve sort of lingered by your side
waiting to hear something too.

All about me were hills
like wide-eyed city skyscrapers
turned friendly and green
simplified without separation
and beckoning me further into the hour.

We turned back soon enough for mother
to catch her breath before dinner and then we slept
in the nightmare of your childhood
until a morning noise brought forth
my body grown much older.

That was a vacation in my poor world
and in this duty, you fulfilled three times
you reminded me a hundred-thousand
times (that you thought would not add up)
that you had no choice but to feed me.

And as I tore through algebra books
and lingered into certain literature
I still couldn't gauge the wind that struck you
each morning anew and awash in the work
that the God your mother worshipped gave you.

In each success that I hung about my neck
like a map of stars or shining teeth
full of glory and the coming of the dawn
even in silly things a child stumbles over
as he's growing, you would not let me have my joy.

And this same burn is in my elbow now
as I take apart this wall, crack this tilted floor,
wrestle this old wire you had me wrestle
during the summers, early in the morning
so, I could make room for a door of black glass.

So, mother could nurse you back to health
after a concrete wall crushed your leg
and Steve could whimper beneath your scowl
and Dan could not mind much
and I could claw out your eyes.

But what's the use since your latest accident
when all the beer in you shifted without warning
and you fell eighteen feet to the concrete
where mother in the kitchen heard you land
with a blow so fierce it should have killed you.

And you who hate hospitals
more than I hate construction
laid up in one for almost two months
after fifty-eight years of near-freedom
that was, no doubt, what drove you mad.

That one day I came to visit you
and you were on drugs I recognized
and you woke from the frozen lung
lying to the doctors who asked you about alcohol
and talking of a cherry pie that didn't exist.

And weeks later you came around
the ribs less purple, the ankle thinner
than a Louisville slugger, and your eyes
filled with a sick water from all the attention
and the fact that you couldn't walk.

I told you about the cherry pie
and I was pulling the damned boards
from the studs as they splintered
and suddenly in this sterile den of family
you had to use the restroom.

You asked me to lift you onto the bed-pan
and subsequently the front wall fell
and for all you had tried to do to me
for twenty-six years, you knew I would lift you gently
though you deliberately put this hate in me.

And as the family watched me hold you
to take a shit I imagined this to be your
moment for that long gallop away from
whatever you might have done different
before what happened to you happened.

I don't know, but what you tried to kill
over breakfast and home-cooked dinner
you needed that day and the doctor's
wouldn't bring you a beer until after
you had reached a certain point.

And without thanks you asked for it
and without grudge I gave it
though poor carpenters overcompensate
with too many nails
just to hold things together.

I tire from fighting them as I think of you
the claw of the hammer at the head
of this bad design, full of air, like your shack
I should rebuild before the winter
when this sheet of night sweat becomes frost.

There is hardly an organ their rusty points
have not struck and turned bitter
or even a drop of blood that is not vinegar
and the only part left is my skin
and it is anxious, looking down.

GIVE MY LOVE TO FATHER

Dementia is a place where you go alone
I say on father's behalf,
because he has never been good with words,
but a man, whom I have told friends
vehemently and viciously that I hate,
I would not have wished this upon.
This is nothing human to go through
as we accept how the body gives way.
Slow down the car crash and watch
the bones of the skull crushing
and a lifetime of visited places, known persons
little flowers grown in the mind of happiness
wilting and withering and shattering against
the invisible glass of the windshield
and spilling into unknown places
from which they will never be found and gathered.
Maps of the streets traveled a thousand times
fading slowly from way out there
and rolled up like an event rug
and coming forever home until
they reach the doorstep to this structure
which has become a mere sandcastle
crumbling from the inside out
and teased into the anonymous waters
of a cold immeasurable ocean.
Surely and daily it drops away
so starkly I have concentrated upon love
that I might painlessly fold my arms around him
and keep away what sifts through all there is
and removes anything but the empty hollow
where he spends most of these,
the so-called golden years.

When he is left alone, five minutes
becomes an unbearable length
and he worries for who is not there
to keep him company and he goes
with his cane, searching for them
or he hunts down the cat
to make sure all which brings him comfort
in the little room where he has gotten
has not gone to stay with the others,
to never return behind those beautiful blue eyes
which set upon me so long ago,
when the world first opened up,
and I, too, knew what nothing was called.

DISTORTED HISTORY

I return to grandmother
on my mother's side who had four children,
two of them by my grandfather who
was away fighter-piloting in World War II—
when, she gave them all away and split town.
He made it through one nightmare and came home
to another—half the world turned off just like that.
I suppose he looked for my mother, her brother,
and even their half-sister and half-brother.
I'm certain he looked for his wife.
The only picture we have of her, black-and-white,
all leggy and thin but with curves
beneath the knee-length skirt.
Though you can't see it, you just know
the full lips are painted red, wetted just then,
when the photographer let her know.

FLAME

ECHO

It is true,
as spring looms this year,
I will sew no more
these seeds of annuals.
Neither potted in the window
for the selfish brick
of morning light,
nor quilted
upon the garden's bed.
I have wept as a lonely drunk
over blooming violet, angel blue,
and freckled red.
I mourn too much
the end of comfort's season.
Yet *and* nonetheless,
I have researched,
(my mind a callous for it),
and found the most exquisite
perennial for the staking.
Dry, dark, quiet even;
I say, worthy of a vault
no shovel's edge
can penetrate.
Tendrils grasping grain,
down deepest,
where winter's frost
fails to crawl.

AFTER THE HOSPITAL

Even seventy feet above
there is no view
from behind the ceiling's curtain.
At the least, not from this
mechanical bed from which
my pricked finger
can give beck to another nurse.
Recalling through the gauze
of these prolonging drugs
very little conjures up beauty
like red flowers drinking rain.
When I am lonely for a field of those,
I go and piss more blood.
It strikes the clear water
and moves like a cloud,
until all light is the very color of it.
It has taken an impressive array
of sickness, like the minutes of a year,
for me to strike out from the desire.
One day, I believe,
I will be captured in another net
of pain that will run
the length of my back.
That, too, will be shouldered
and this moment just passed,
unregistered on the chart
of the double-plugged monitor,
—this moment so full of dumb joy—
I want to call my mother,
and tell her how this sap
I'll call a soul has been tapped
from the bark of my slow dying.

AN IMMENSE WAITING

Three times I have nearly died
and come to an earlier end.
There was the time in '86
at the 60mph whim
of forces which move stars
while behind the wheel of that Ranger
and managed a sidelong dive
into some hollowed out and nameless ditch
which pitched the truck over twice
through a rising field of corn
and managed only to demolish
the truck and one-hundred fifty square feet of crop
through which the blasted
wreckage traveled before
jolting to a shocked stillness
upright on four good tires.
I remember a scream raked over a metal throat,
the popping of a glass balloon,
before, alive, I fell into the farmer's dust
and took account of the midnight sky:
bruises splashed across an endless canvas.
Then in 2002, of all times,
six full months after
I'd quit drinking for good,
I got mired into the darkest place
like a black knot on a cherry tree.
I drove my car across the backyard
one October Sunday afternoon
and parked it at the tree line,
and brought an old 1-inch rubber tubing
leftover from remaking the buried cistern,
and I taped it to the tailpipe,

then snaked it through the back window
like a giant S waiting to close up
and fall on its side into infinity
as I had some beautiful music playing
that I would mangle into a death march
as I sat there feeling smaller than
an empty watchpocket
on a cheap pair of old jeans.
Then comes along, on my dead-end
driveway a couple hundred yards long,
and out of nowhere this minivan
I suppose looking for a place to turn around
out there in the picturesque thousands of acres
decorating the hills slung about the southern edge
of the county with a million trees in metamorphosis,
and it excites my godsend of a dog,
my big gray-black mutt with the purple tongue
who was undoubtedly camped at the back door
through which I'd gone missing,
and I hear him over the music
barking that low guttural beastly call
older than the stones at the base of pyramids,
and he just kept on going
long after the minivan had found its way
and into the next song and the next
with his inarticulate lament,
and I couldn't turn that fucking key in the ignition
and leave him there to be taken care
by some other soul than the one inside of me.
Five years from that ordeal
finds me in the white dream of a hospital bay,
dazed from months of not-knowing,
and just embodied by a general stupor
as the whole cloth remade of fatigue
in tiny little stitches of sickness

put into me through the needle's eye,
when, with no ado to be spoken of,
my heart goes flat quick as light
cast out from an eye closed shut,
and everything had an eerie numbness
that was neither tactile nor otherwise,
a glimpse not quite of absence at the edge
of an immense waiting yet held at bay,
and the doctors all rushed in and
shooshed the family along to the corridor,
and the MDs fed me a good helping
of hard looks and electricity and *boom!*
My heart wakes up,
wet leaves of greenery in a rain forest.

SHEER WHITE

I want to tell you about my simple house.
About the cinder wall-stones I carried out one by one.
The labor of re-shaping it as my own.
I want to tell you about a yew I planted.
The snow on its whiskers.
A fence I built between the yard and road.
But a train wails beside my desk chair.
There is a violent gasp of an avalanche about me.
And suddenly people have no skin.
It is terrifying to be one of them.
Displaced nights of no rhythm.
The pink cut of the horizon.
Then a dawn that never breaks into sun.
A display of trapped blood.
A placenta dried and light as dragonfly wings.
That nightmare of the times I couldn't scream.
A sheer white pass in the shadow of a shadow.
A young man seeing himself old and almost gone.

SKELETON

There is no place here for cars or planes.
No space on the wall for clocks.
But all the world for movement and for time.
Destroy all the streetlights,
the microwaves, and calculators.
Bury the wreckage in fiction and song.
Here, there is moon and fire and thought.
Level all houses and chisel away the streets
with tools made of naught but bone.
There are no clear paths.
Our skin is a home.
There is no place for cultivated flowers,
zoos, arboretums, or house beloved pets.
Only the stark and honest wild.
(A truly hungry cat would kill me in my sleep.)
There are places for death and murder,
and a panorama built of color.
But sink your computer.
The only internet is God.
There is a fish consuming boats and barges
in his ichthus imagination as vast as sky,
and less room, yet, to occupy.
For there is no place for jazz, or poetry,
painting, sculpture, theatre.
It tears me like a saw to let them go.
I would sacrifice even my only true love,
language, for one dim star's soul.

SLOWLY

Slowly, by the slightest inklings,
I turn more and mostly into water.
Objects I once grasped upon
do not so much as slip through
my simply human hands,
but my fingers shatter across them
unsettled and silky they slip about
the other side, the far side
to gather once again where my arms end,
and it is not just my hands
but my feet and my legs,
and my head and my heart,
all slowly, irrevocably turning into water
that comes asunder against
the slightest interruptive intrusion
to this gentle inner hold
about which I no longer resist
nor scorn, nor laugh.
Without reservation, a thought
drops away ten tons of shadow,
and it rips through me, and I shatter
harmlessly, and into the low air
of this house, my bedroom hallway
somewhere along the sidewalk
I might happen to be in life,
and I ride gravity into the low spot
to find myself gathered and whole;
a puddle, if you will, but something
through which light passes and a thin surface
reflecting the sky.

VEINS

Daily they were mined in the hospital.
Harvested by industrial machination,
sterile thin and glaring like chrome.
Before the plunge I could see myself
unshaven, lost muscle, extra fat, and
my tired medicinally stoned eyes...
the facsimile of my dried-together lips,
my long head wrapped around the needle.
The rubbery tourniquet tied off at the bicep,
before the registered hands held me;
"Pump your fist, okay." Then,
the tap of the two agile fingers like code
across an intermediary wall of conjoined cells,
the breath-quiet asking, "Are you there?"
Something she would gaze towards,
a lapidary of viscous gems, flowing through
me in the gray light of overcast windows,
something pulsing, regulated and measured
by unintelligible design.
There in the vampiric hull I saw myself,
indeed, I saw a hundred million years implode,
and though I was fed liquid during the genesis
of my disease, though I could close my vision
and see the blue where she would aim her dart,
always, always it morphed red before my open eyes,
and then the white ceiling of no account.

VEINS II

Blue rivers in their ancient beds,
what makes its way beneath the flesh
eats through bone and stone,
yet breaks in two beneath a touch.
Tapped by needles, stopped by dykes,
this contradiction can just suffice
to trap the air and air alike
to feed the fish and sooth the heart.
The cold so deep where black's the sea,
no current moves the stolid algae,
fine as filament, soft again as sympathy.

VEINS III

No vein grows which does not consume
the light which pushes out forever
from the carcinogen so tethered.
The racing heart made alarm
as if the big sun were fading
along the corridors to Pluto.
Down in my right limb
the fourth toe has quit.
Sometimes a tingling
bites flesh and bone
or pain I will stand...
Light pushes far beyond
where medicine
seems to reach,
or the eye
seems to
see.

FLAME

I was told once that poetry
is about the language
and it stuck for decades
but while it is certainly
impossible without the chosen,
an eighth-grade insult
is also about the language.
Now, I won't say that
some mother-fucker lied
to me about poetry
but maybe, like cells in a fingertip,
there were too many ways
of going about poetry
to count them all
and you lose people,
even hungry students and learners,
when you say *soul*.
Soul, like poetry,
is always insufficient;
there are not enough letters
to truly spell *soul*
and both soul and poetry
are ultimately too tiny
for the thing itself.
Many aspects of a rich life
become deficient when
defined by language.
What of silence?
You see, it is better to say
poetry is a flower
which has a green stem
and the stem has roots

and there is dirt and soil
and light falls from on high
which awakens the systemic whole
and petals reach for the sky,
for other petals, for the nearest water
and the roots crawl, also, towards water
as life is impossible without water.
Life is about water more than
poetry is about language
but I am only musing on this
because I hate poems
about poetry.
They never do "it" for me.
Certainly not like tonight
when I turned off all the lights
upstairs here where
one of my legs is slowly dying
and I have lost all fear of death
so much so that I've realized
sight is most notable
to a closed eye.
And when the lights were all off,
like closing the eye to this room,
I lit a scented candle
with its wick delving up from
a plug of red handcrafted wax
and I put some Mingus on the speakers
and turned it up just right
before I fell back into
the chair and comfort
and I forgot all that I have known
as the flame danced to jazz
as if it, too, wanted to get away
from that which kept it grounded.

BEFORE THE GRAVE,

poetry is the final extract of life.
I sit like a cape of hours
upon me as wings,
the sweat of the day tangled
into the fabric of this shirt,
my socks filled with a ghost-
the half-truths married with centuries,
little decades, moments kissing the arm raised
and the blinking of this bloodshot eye.
I see so little I drown in one single breath
and upon me comes
the weight of all light.
I am smothered.
Plainspoken as the rain
which shreds the very air.
Thought itself becomes
a delicacy of danger.
Little tools prying loose
from a cornucopia of rock
and chiseled into shape
by fabric soft as water
until precious stones spill loose
and into the mind
sprouts this succulent dance.
This is pure communication
with the unbreakable silence
sitting alone; a stone
beneath the saturation of gravity
imperceptivity cut along what is ever-passing.
All my corners are smoothed over—
so much so that I am eternally undaunted.
The rope runs through me drawn taut.

I speak in a language unto nothing
but the stark green trees,
the weeds pushed up through
the stony happenstance of this all.
I reach toward the only known light.
Muted words chosen most carefully.
They are abstractly me.
So much so that I admit to tumors.
One-offs into the vast
bucket of shadows.
I go down exactly like
any given sunset
when mountains crumble
into shadows.

EPILOGUE

After having dreamed of being a poet
and becoming one
all becomes a dream
until it settles like a sleepy quiet
over the skin of time
the magic held together
gathered in a jar

AFTERWORD
by Kent Fielding

During the winter of 2000-2001, D.S. Poorman (David Scott Baker) and I crisscrossed the state of Kentucky many times with a big metal book, *The Book of Kentucky*, collecting handwritten literature from Kentucky's greatest living writers. One of these trips is briefly recounted in the poem, "Kent":

> And how funny this moment now
> as we ride together for ten hours this gray Sunday
> with a metal book of blank pages
> we will fill one by one.

That moment symbolized our friendship. We traveled together in various ways throughout its course. That morning, that Sunday, we had just visited James Still in the small town of Hazard in southeastern Kentucky, a four-hour drive from Louisville. James Still was 96 and we found him in a cabin with a blanket over his legs, watching a University of Kentucky basketball game. Upon entering, I apologized for interrupting his game. He replied, "They aren't playing well." When he looked at the metal book—it weighed over 20 pounds—he said, "Now, I understand." He meant the purpose behind the book. "I didn't quite get what it was in your letter." After he wrote a poem in the book, he began talking of World War II and how he survived a plane crash in Cairo that killed most of his platoon. He finished with "That's the first time I ever talked about that moment." James Still entered the war as a non-commissioned officer (perhaps a corporal) even though he had a master's degree and had already published his best-known book, *Rivers of the Earth* (1939). He claimed not to like "officers" and wanted to be with the common soldier. James Still died a month after our visit. Those were the moments D.S. and I shared—gathering not only poems, but conversations—meeting people. We left Hazard and drove another two hours to visit Kenneth King outside of Pikesville Kentucky. He seemed to live in the middle of a barren field in a house that looked out on flat farmland, probably tobacco in the summer. He said, "I get the page next to James Still!" He jumped around and danced in celebration.

There were many other trips with *The Book of Kentucky*. There was the trip out to Iowa to visit Chris Offutt during a massive snowstorm and with the band, Art Cannon, who hummed and sang as we drove. We had to stop outside of Peoria because of the snow, a white out, and ate at a drive-through taco shop. During that trip Chris Offutt made the joke, "I'm going to start publishing all my manuscripts in big 20-pound metal books." There was the trip to New Orleans to visit the writer/critic T.R. Johnson. We stayed at his house in the French Quarter and talked about Kentucky writers; about Hunter S. Thompson typing *The Great Gatsby* so he could get the feel of Fitzgerald's sentences into his blood; about T.R.'s memories of his good friend, the poet, Brett Ralph; even about Daniel Boone.

As D.S. says in his poem, "Kent," we went our separate ways only to come back together to finish some uncompleted task: "And each/ saw our return to some central purpose, a reason that brought us back and said that we were not finished/ with this sophisticated spin."

That sophisticated spin has brought me to this book.

*

D.S. Poorman (David Scott Baker, known to almost everyone as Dave) and I became friends running cross-country together in high school. His poem "Running" references this time. We were both good runners and the team was both successful and incredibly close. Like many cross-country teams, we appeared to be outcasts and overachievers. We ran in meets in the woods and mountains of Kentucky and traveled yearly to the state meet, one of the few teams at Waggener High School to qualify yearly for the Kentucky State Championship. The team produced a 3-time college All-American runner (David Keyes), three lawyers, a few writers, and even (on the girls' team) the actor Kira Reed. Even in high school Dave was writing poetry, openly, and he was incredibly confident in his talent, incredibly confident in nearly everything he did. I want to stress that being a poet and a cross-country runner didn't necessarily put you in the "in-crowd," and people in high school disliked Dave because he was creative, independent, and cocky. During this time Dave had created the cross-country team's flag which we took to all our meets. On it was the team slogan he had coined: "Milers Keep It Up Longer." For some reason the coach never said anything about it. Dave also started rapping, sometimes at opposing teams: "You're looking at me 'cause I spit in your eye/ your momma told me that I'm her best guy."

During this time, as a team, we did things like crash rival schools' parties, and hang out in the kitchen, and when no-one was around, we'd steal all the beer and alcohol in the refrigerator and scram. One particular night this almost got us into a fight with some members of Trinity's cross-country team. I believe someone had driven by and shouted some profanity at us after we left. I remember Dave leading the sprint down the street, back towards the house we had just left, ready to smash someone's face.

Of course, Dave claimed, at the time, to be all about love.

*

After high school, Dave went to the University of Western Kentucky in Bowling Green. He majored in journalism, but left after two years. I went to the University of Louisville where I eventually became co-editor of *Thinker Review* and co-founder of White Fields Press and its umbrella nonprofit, *the literary renaissance*. I later moved to Fairbanks and earned an MFA in Poetry at the University of Alaska Fairbanks. Dave bought a condemned house at the top of Jefferson Forest in Fairdale, Kentucky and began to create a growing body of writing. The house in Jefferson Forest reflected his most tranquil years. Many of the nature poems in this book stem from Dave's life in that house. During this time period, Dave and I, when we saw each other, were mostly close drinking partners, and we took drinking trips together. During one trip, we found ourselves in the mountains of Colorado at some bar—I want to say in the town of Drake—at 4 p.m. We had met two girls and were drinking and conversing with them when around midnight Dave, who had a fondness for bourbon, lost the ability to communicate. One of the girls, said, "I guess Dave's watching tonight." At 4 a.m., I awoke in the back of his van parked outside of a closed camp ground—it was April and cold—with Dave next to me. I don't know how we got there, but I heard a wolf howl. There was another trip to New York, where after leaving the bar we spent hours riding up and down Manhattan on the subway because Dave wanted to people watch. He was fascinated with people in subways and would say things like, "Look at her. Look at her. I wonder what she does for a living. What does she read at night? I wonder if she has a boyfriend?" We finally ended up at a friend of a friend of a friend's apartment. I had no idea who she was but she was nice enough to give us her bed, to which Dave immediately took off all his clothes in front of her and said something like, "Don't worry I do this all the time." She did make us coffee and eggs in the morning, so I guess she wasn't too upset.

Dave went sober in 2002, and a few of the poems in this book deal with his addiction to alcohol, his recovery, and sobriety. He claimed to have almost drunk himself to death, and I remember watching him once drink two shots of bourbon at 8 a.m. just to get out of the house. He had entered that room where drinking was no longer fun; the relationship had turned abusive: "I was drinking a fifth of bourbon every day and shitting blood," he said. J.D. Daniels, a writer from Louisville, suggests that drinking that much is like getting beat-up nightly. Another time, after an event at some bar with a group of friends, Dave pretended to hug his whiskey glass and said, "Jim Beam is my real friend, the rest of you are just acquaintances." It was a joke, but a joke with some truth.

*

In the summer of 2000, after both Dave and I had read at the Boston Poetry Festival, we drove to Montreal to visit the writer Ryan Masters. We were out exploring the famous mountains of Montreal. Not far from the top, a cemetery was stretched with old white markers bearing dates of a previous century. They had buried the dead near the sky so they could be closer to God (the trees and the sky both held quiet sentry over the graves). We turned on a dirt path and as an out of control bicycle passed us with an old man, bald with gray sideburns, singing in French. We jumped out of the man's way to avoid being hit and climbed under a group of Hawthorne and up onto the stone battlement of a fort-turned-park and looked out over ancient Montreal, a rustic city of old brick architecture and modern skyscrapers surrounded by water. Here, at the top of Mt. Royal, peace had been arranged between the Native Americans and the French. As we looked out, the rivers seemed to meditate and cradle Montreal on its shoulders. I asked D.S., "Would you like to help me organize an Insomniacathon?"

"Sure," he said. "What would its reason be?'

During the hike, we'd been talking about two ninety-year-old women in Alaska who were the last speakers of a language and when they died a whole universe would go extinct. Communication was the creation of worlds and the beginning of art. We wanted to do something that would capture a moment in our time to preserve our own language that might suddenly or slowly disappear.

That, of course, was the defining, internal reason. The other, external reason would be the Franciscan Shelter House in downtown Louisville. The Franciscan Shelter House, at the time, had been serving 250-300 meals per day to the poor of Louisville for 29 years. They needed to rebuild as their building had been condemned. The city could not afford to lose such an institution. Both directors, Bro. James Fields and Bro. Ray Ramos, worked for room and board. They received no salary. Dave and I believed that art could make a difference in people's lives, and we believed that art could make a difference in a community. An event could rise money to help the homeless.

That Mt. Royal hike spawned two ideas: Insomniacathon and *The Book of Kentucky*. We would use the latter to fund the former. The idea was taken from Theo Dougan's *Book of Ireland*, which sold for $2,000,000. I thought a book representing Kentucky's rich literature could raise the necessary funds to put on the event.

Dave commissioned Matt Davis of Rust Brothers to build the book. On Sunday Oct. 28th, they picked out a piece of metal for the cover that was lying beside a barn on the Rust Brothers' 20-acre property in Salem, Indiana. Inside the house of the old Amish dairy farm they sat over dinner and drew out the design. Three days later Matt

Davis had a heart attack outside of Cahoots, a bar on Bardstown Road, and passed away. Matt had been one of Dave's closest friends since college and Dave went crazy for nearly a week. Finally, Joe Werth, Matt's roommate and fellow Rust Brother, agreed to finish the book based on Matt's designs.

According to my email records, we started organizing Insomniacathon 2001 on September 12, 2000. Our first task was to find a headliner, a name that would draw a crowd. I made a long list of writers: Gregory Corso, Clarence Majors, Michael Waters, Amiri Baraka, David Lee, E. Ethelbert Miller, Anne Waldman, Jean Valentine, Gil Scott-Heron, Sonia Sanchez and so on. I first called Lawrence Ferlinghetti.

"I don't want to commit to anything that far in advance," he said. "I'm an old man. Send me a letter."

After a brief discussion of the event, we talked about fees. I knew Ferlinghetti charged a healthy sum.

"I have an agent in New York," he said, "that gets me $5000 a reading, but that's for people I don't know or don't like. For you guys $2000. Send me a letter and I'll think about it."

We eventually settled on poet, activist, and musician Ed Sanders, author of *Tales of Beatnik Glory*, *1968: A History in Verse* and *A Poem from Jail*. Sanders was the founder of the Fugs and edited the counter-culture magazine *Fuck-You: A Journal of the Arts*. We also brought in younger writers such as the Palestinian poet Suheir Hummad, Lee Ann Brown, and Sean Cole. The event would last over 82 non-stop hours and feature over 150 poets, over 100 bands, theatre groups, jugglers, comedians, and puppeteers. It would be the largest poetry/music festival in Kentucky history.

Insomniacathon 2001 began with a reading at Presentation Academy in downtown Louisville not far from the

Franciscan Shelter House. The reading featured some high school poets and D.S. Poorman. At the time, my sister taught at Presentation and was worried about what Dave might say. "Make sure he doesn't say anything stupid." Dave showed up late and hungover. His novel, *Macky Dunn's Got Nothing to Lose*, had recently been published and during his reading/talk he kept repeating, "Now the name of my book is *Macky Dunn's Got Nothing to Lose*." He said this about five times. At the end, during question and answer, some girl at the back of the room raised her hand and mocked, "What's the name of your book again?" Dave, laughing the entire time, wrote the name on the blackboard. "*Macky Dunn's Got Nothing to Lose*," he shouted. We still had 80-hours of the Insomniacathon to go.

I remember Dave telling me, months later, how he drove down to the Franciscan House, paced back and forth outside the building before going in, and when he handed the check to Bro. James Fields, said, "This is a donation from all the artists in Louisville." Bro. James looked at the check and his eyes widened. "Thank you!" he said. "And bless you and all the artists." It was one of Dave's proudest memories.

But in September 2000 (quoting my intro to Insomniacathon), "Little did either of us know that the event, Insomniacathon 2001, would have us crisscrossing the state eight, nine, ten times—sometimes all day, sometimes in the middle of the night—gathering handwritten prose and poems in a big metal book weighing over twenty pounds, or driving out into a blizzard of the mid-west to hunt out Chris Offutt or driving down into the heart of the South to stand in front of Eudora Welty's lawn or discuss Daniel Boone in the French Quarter with T.R. Johnson. Neither of us realized that we'd spend hours debating schedules, bands, egos, Insomniacathon Stout, that we'd almost come to blows when all our free time disappeared into meetings, phone calls, emails, driving, or that we'd learn a great deal about homelessness in Louisville and make it our cause, or experience the death of a friend. Insomniacathon 2001 became a creature of its own...living, breathing, demanding, and with a vast spiritual life and understanding. As the poet James Baker Hall said about *The Book of Kentucky* (but in a sense about the entire event), "There's a great deal of karma in this book."

*

After Insomniacathon 2001, I moved back to Alaska to teach at the boarding school Mt. Edgecumbe, but Dave and I continued to "return" to our friendship to finish "some central purpose" because we were not finished with our travels.

After Dave quit drinking he began to craft and perfect handmade books. In 2005, he created *The Book of America* and we embarked on a journey to fill it with two poets from every state. The idea was that as we filled the book we would write a guidebook to famous literary sites in America, and a memoir about the experience. One trip had us at Howard University at E. Ethelbert Miller's office in the school's library. There Dave and Ethelbert debated baseball. Ethelbert was an Ichiro Suzuki fan, and would travel to Seattle every summer, buying seats behind right field, so he could watch what Ichiro did in the outfield. Ethelbert claimed that Icharo performed magic between pitches, little things, the language of his body, the bounce of his toes, the concentration in the face—like poetry. Dave, as a young boy, was a well-known little league pitcher, and the two got into a heated debate that finally delved into baseball and sci-fi. "What if," Ethelbert posed, "a pitcher had a reconstructed arm that made him stronger and gave him an advantage?" Note, these were the days of steroids and homerun records being set year after year, and so the question had some merit in reality.

"Like a bionic arm?"

"Yeah, like science advances to a place where they can make someone stronger, or parents can genetically engineer a child for features that would make him a better athlete. Would that be unfair, should that be against what the major league allows?"

"Yes, but if it sells tickets, the league and media would go for it. We all want superheroes."

"But it would turn everyone into spectators. Sports would be for the wealthy and the elite."

That trip had us visiting Antietam (wondering about the battle and the dead), camping out at Greenbelt National Park, listening to bluegrass, eating cheap Chinese food, and reading poetry to each other. Dave often wrote while I drove, and I often told him about Alaska as he drove: "There was this one time in late May when I was running up Mt. Roberts behind Juneau, and I got close to the mountain top and the trail disappeared under snow. I stopped running to try figure out where the trail was, and I look up and not twenty yards from me was this brown bear standing on its hind legs sniffing the air. I thought, "Oh shit, I'm dead."

Other trips with the *The Book of America* included traveling to Delaware to have coffee with Fleda Brown. She talked about writing a book of poetry about Elvis, or the obsession of Elvis, while Dave talked about writing a book of poetry about the history of bluegrass music (this book was never written but one poem "On the Radio After the Storm" in this book survives). Another trip included travel to Virginia to seek out Edgar Allen Poe sites (one of Dave's favorite writers) and to meet with Rita Dove and Charles Wright at the University of Virginia.

The Book of America is housed at the University of Louisville Library, but remains unfinished.

*

As a writer, Dave often said that "As an editor, Kent, you are invaluable." To which, I often chuckled or laughed outright. Sometimes this laughter offended Dave. "I'm serious," he would say. Dave had a hard time letting anyone edit his work, and sometimes he threw away entire manuscripts, entire novels, based on editing comments and his desire not to rewrite something according to my directions. For example, below is a poem Dave used to send out to magazines with his poetry (that is, until he stopped sending his work out):

To You Who Judge My Poems
(A note on submissions)
Okay, it is a pedantic note,
Insipid at best, but nonetheless,
I thought of it all on my own.
I thought that I did not like
The idea of you, gentle sirs
And gentle ladies, circled at a
Round table to judge my helpless poems.

I have not thought much of thoughts
Convened and arrived at round-tables
Round the world. So, if you would,
And I ask so humbly, please, take each
A copy and move off to a corner by
Your beautifully competent self
If you have not done so, already.

As a writer, Dave also had the habit of sending me work at the craziest of times, and had a habit, that once he started writing a manuscript, he wrote non-stop for days, weeks, even months, and as an editor, I often had to keep up with his pace for Dave, during his creativity, would get impatient without feedback, and often do rash things—like create marquees announcing his new book and put the marquee in the back of his truck and drive around town promoting it (I even imagined him with a megaphone shouting out his truck window, "Go buy D.S. Poorman's new novel"); or, even worse, send out a first draft to a publisher. He often admitted how much he hated rewriting.

I remember being in a production of *Much Ado About Nothing* in Sitka, and being backstage between sets marking up a manuscript. The director even asked, "What are you doing? Aren't you in the next scene?" And I replied, "I'm editing." The director threw up his hands, "What the fuck?" Or, teaching in the Marshall Islands and spending most of the night, sometimes all night, making comments on *Once Removed*, and fueled with coffee that next day, I'd often talk about the book and about writing with my classes. One day one of my students said, "Mr. Fielding, you know how to promote a book. I'd like to read whatever you're editing. Who is this D.S. Poorman guy anyway?"

When David Scott Baker died in 2019, Joel Halbleib, a college friend of Dave's, sent a file with all of the writing he had backed up for Dave in 2015 or 2016. Steven Baker, Dave's brother, sent me all of Dave's recent work that was on Dave's computer, and Dave's mom mailed me all his uncollected papers. Dave had written well over a thousand poems, but they were all saved alphabetically and covered thirty years of his life. He left no outline for a planned book or what he wanted done with his poems, and I spent a year reading the poems, editing the poems, and putting them into some thematic structure: one that seemed to be his autobiography. There was an unspoken agreement between us that I would put out Dave's last book—our last adventure together. Some of the poems in this book, Dave would have never published while alive, and some of the poems in this book are edited and cut (things that maybe

Dave would not have allowed me to do). I found poems hidden under stories. Poems that seemed to be parts of longer poems but were left unfinished. Poems that were handwritten but never typed. Poems that he seemed to hide. He was always writing, but not always putting things in a place where they could be saved or seen. This book went through many drafts and transformations. I had long conversations with various friends and writers including Laura Loran, Ryan Masters, Mark Forman, Jennifer Seelig, Krista Kane and perhaps others who I may have briefly forgotten. They were all instrumental in shaping this book, and they were all important in Dave's life. I cut poems from this book that I love because either they didn't fit, or the section they fit in was too long, or structurally the poem didn't work or contained words that maybe an older, wiser, Dave would not have used. Perhaps these works will appear someplace later. Perhaps not.

At the end of the poem, "Kent", D.S. has me ask him, "What are you going to do with your poems?"
    He responds: "I thought I made that clear years ago.
    I'm going to love you with them until we're home."

Dave, my good friend, we are home.

ABOUT THE AUTHOR

D.S. Poorman, the pen name of David Scott Baker, published three novels during his life, *Macky Dunn's Got Nothing to Lose* (1999), *Once Removed* (2011), and *Somewhere There's A Place* (2014). A woodcraftsman and a book smith, D.S. designed and crafted wooden books, including the *The Largest Poetry Book in the World*, and *The Book of America* (an unfinished project that was to collect handwritten poems by poets across the country). Many of his wooden books have been collected by the University of Louisville's Ekstrom Library Rare Book Collection.

D.S. and Kent Fielding produced and hosted Insomniacathon 2001, the largest music/poetry festival in Kentucky history, lasting over eighty-two non-stop hours and featuring over 150 poets and 100 bands. The festival raised money for the Franciscan Shelter House in downtown Louisville. D.S. Poorman and Kent Fielding also edited *The Book of Kentucky* (2001), a large metal book weighting twenty pounds, containing handwritten poems by many of Kentucky's best-known writers. *The Book of Kentucky* is also housed at Ekstrom Library.

D.S. Poorman claimed to write his poetry late at night and rarely sent his work out. He died in 2019. This is his first collection of poetry.

www.ingramcontent.com/pod-product-compliance
Lightning Source LLC
Chambersburg PA
CBHW030440010526
44118CB00011B/724